CREATION

Enjoy God's Presence + the Beauty of all around you.

joJSKY

Genesis 1:1–31, 2:1–4
(The New American Bible)

Joanne M. Semancik Krenicky Yarsevich

With Illustration by

joSKY

ISBN 978-1-64114-680-7 (Paperback)
ISBN 978-1-64114-682-1 (Hard Cover)
ISBN 978-1-64114-681-4 (Digital)

Scripture texts in this work are taken from the *New American Bible with Revised New Testament* © 1986, 1970 Confraternity of Christian Doctrine, Washington, D.C. and are used by permission of the copyright owner. All Rights Reserved. No part of the New American Bible may be reproduced in any form without permission in writing from the copyright owner.

Copyright © 2017 by Joanne M. Semancik Krenicky Yarsevich
All rights reserved. No part of this publication may be reproduced, distributed, or transmitted in any form or by any means, including photocopying, recording, or other electronic or mechanical methods without the prior written permission of the publisher. For permission requests, solicit the publisher via the address below.

Christian Faith Publishing, Inc.
296 Chestnut Street
Meadville, PA 16335
www.christianfaithpublishing.com

Printed in the United States of America

I dedicate this book, *Creation*, to the following:

Sr. Celine, O.S.F., School Sisters of St. Francis

Sts. Cyril and Methodius Catholic Church, Bethlehem, Pennsylvania;

My grandchildren Anna Grozier, Freyja June, and Gavin Lee;

To those who follow in order to recognize the presence of God in their lives.

GOD Is LOVE!

In the beginning, darkness covered the abyss. God said, "Let there be light."

God called the light "day" and the darkness God called "night."

God saw how good the light was.

Evening came, and morning followed- The first day.

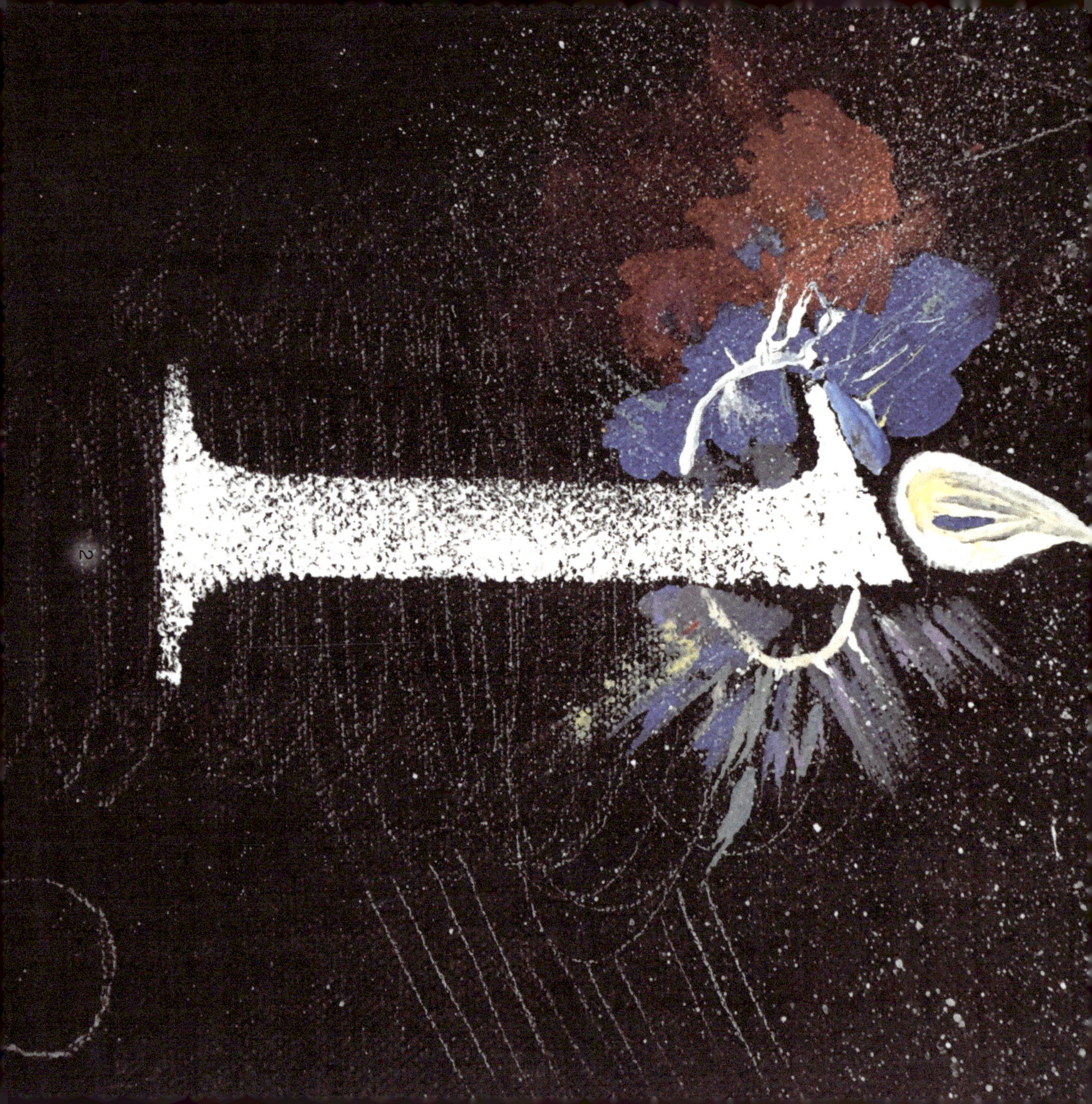

Draw and color your own ideas!

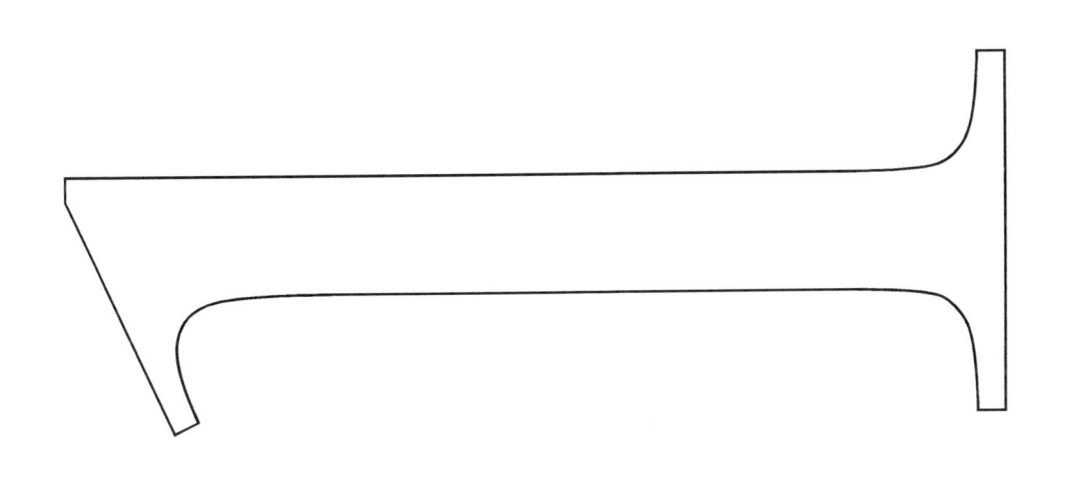

God said, "Let there be a dome in the middle of the waters..."
God called the dome "the sky."
Evening came, and morning followed-
The second day.

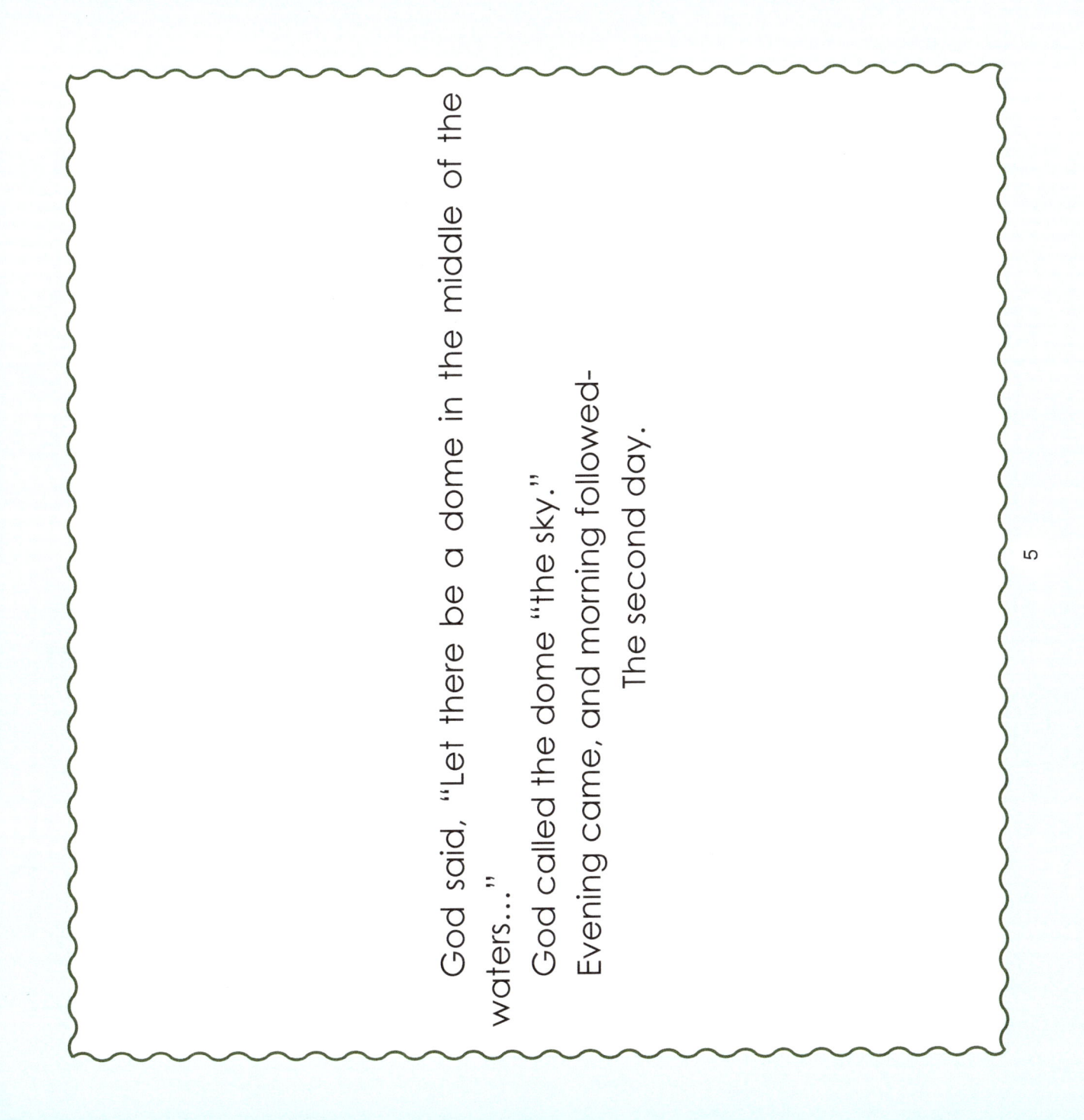

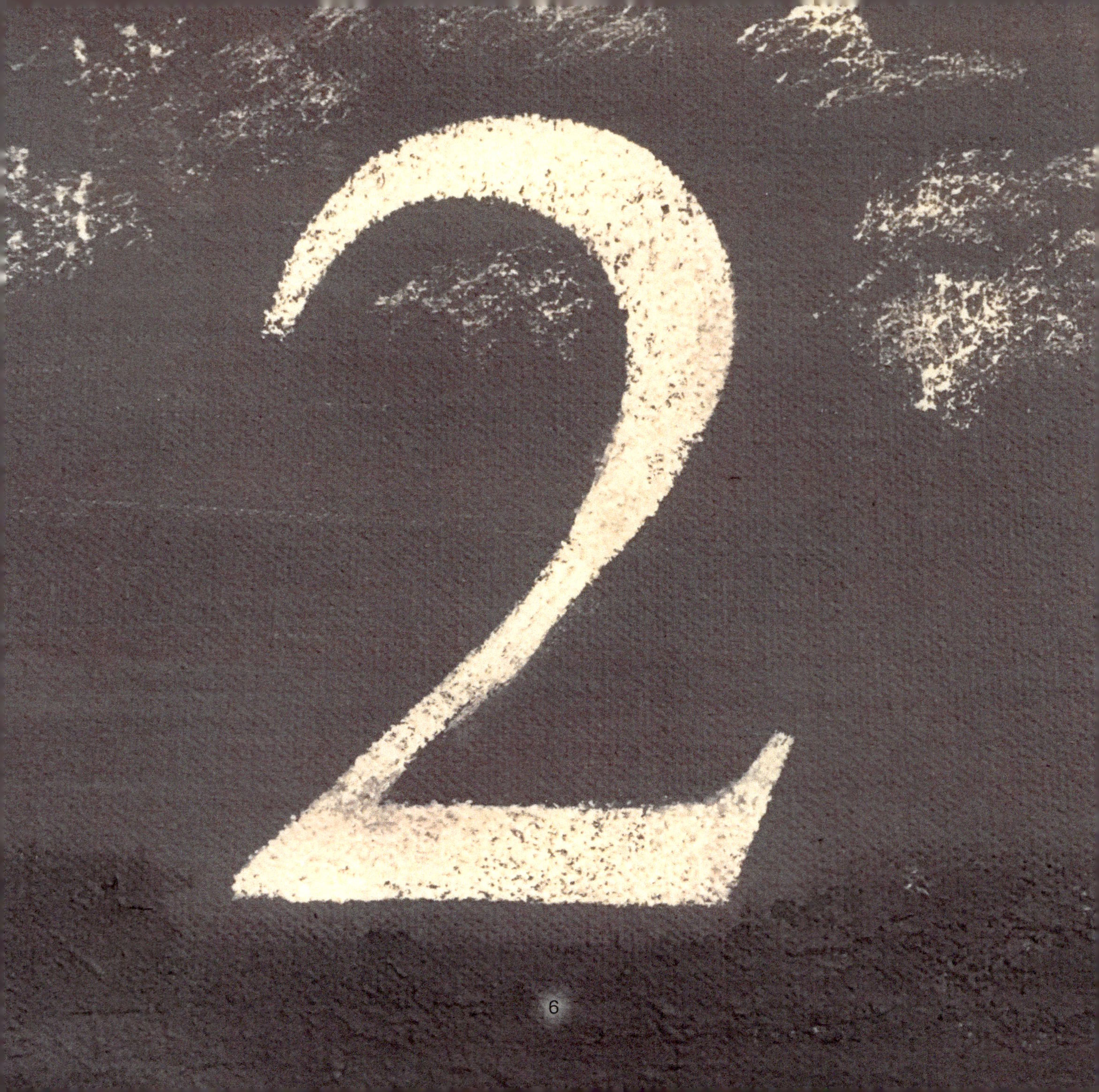
2

Draw and color your own ideas!

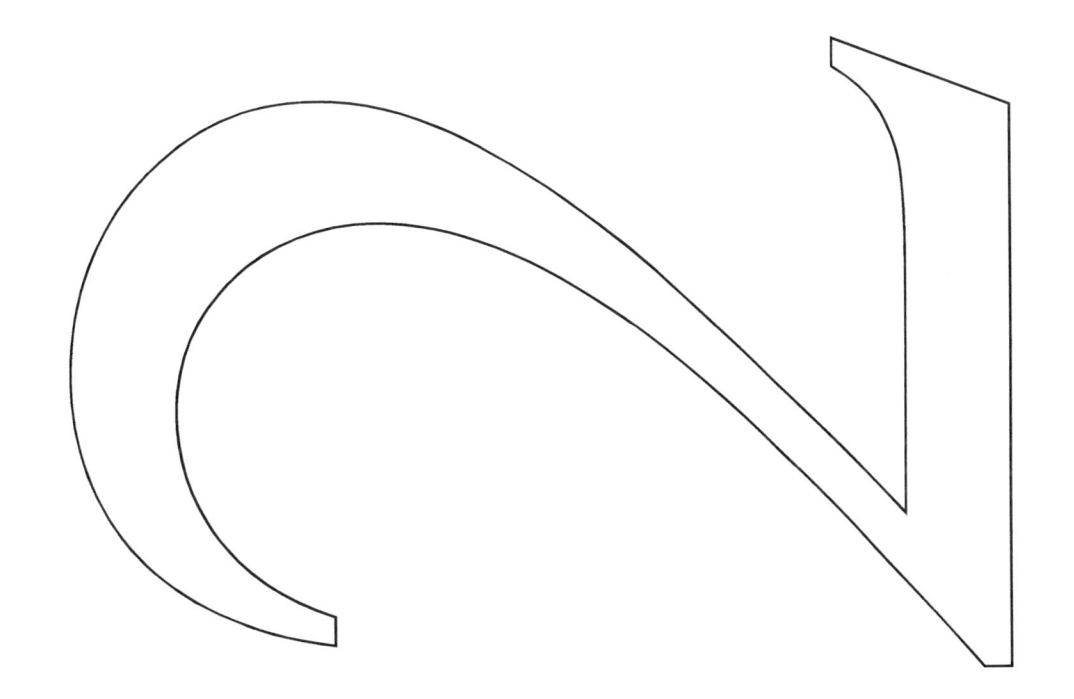

Then God said, "Let the water under the sky be... in a single basin so that dry land may appear."
God called the dry land "the earth."
The basin of the water, God called "the sea."
Then God said, "Let the earth bring forth vegetation: every kind of plant that bears seed and every kind of fruit tree on earth that bears fruit with its seed in it."
God saw how good it was.
Evening came, and morning followed-
The third day.

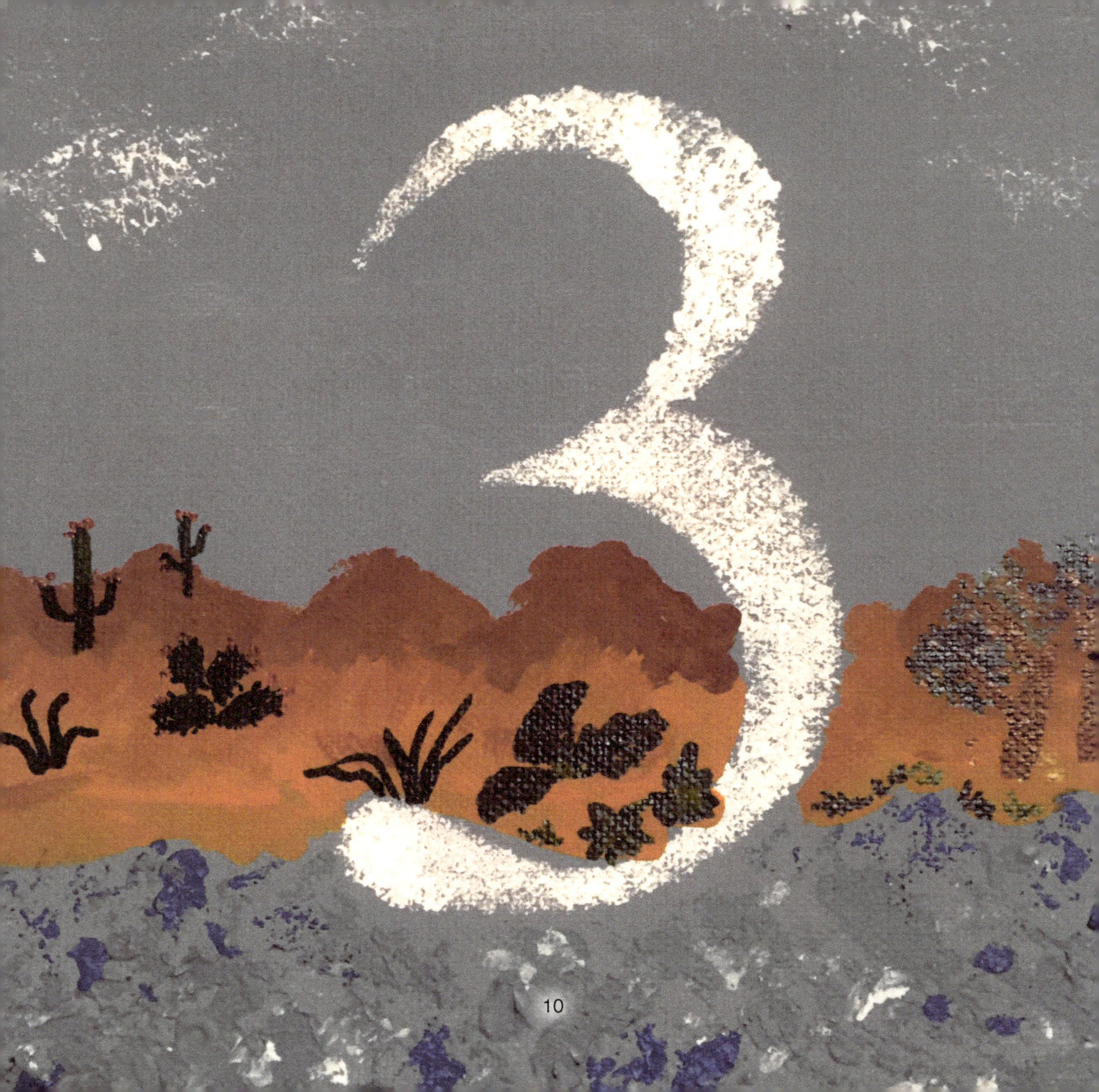
3

Draw and color your own ideas!

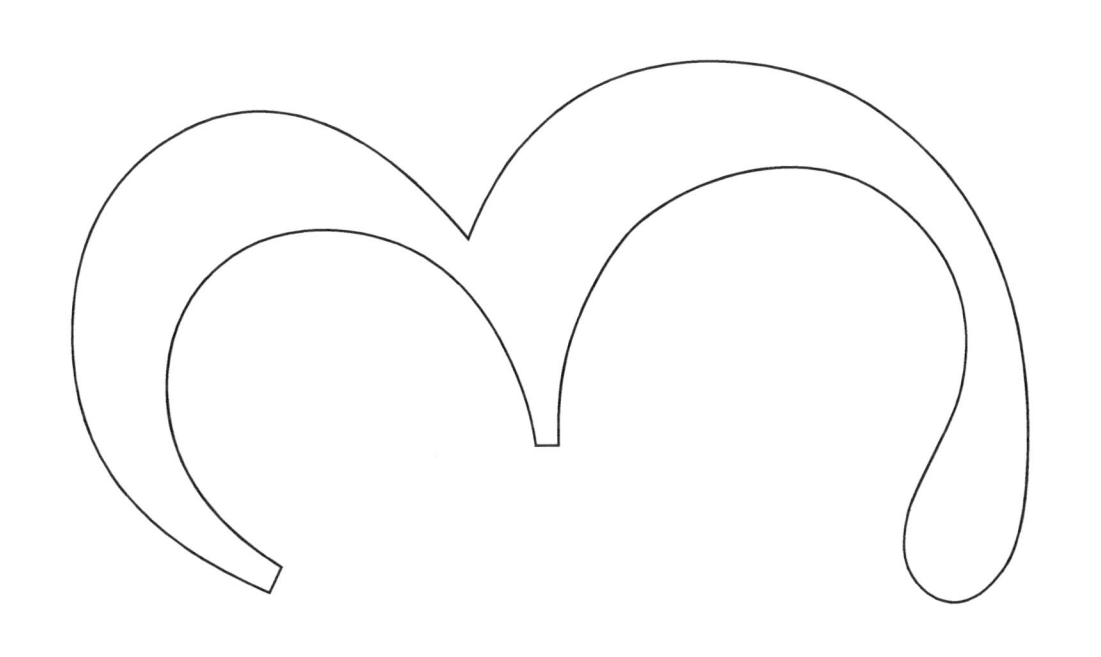

Then God said, "Let there be lights in the dome of the sky, to separate day from night."

God made two great lights: the greater one to govern the day, the lesser one to govern the night; And God made the stars.

Evening came, and morning followed-
The fourth day.

14

Draw and color your own ideas!

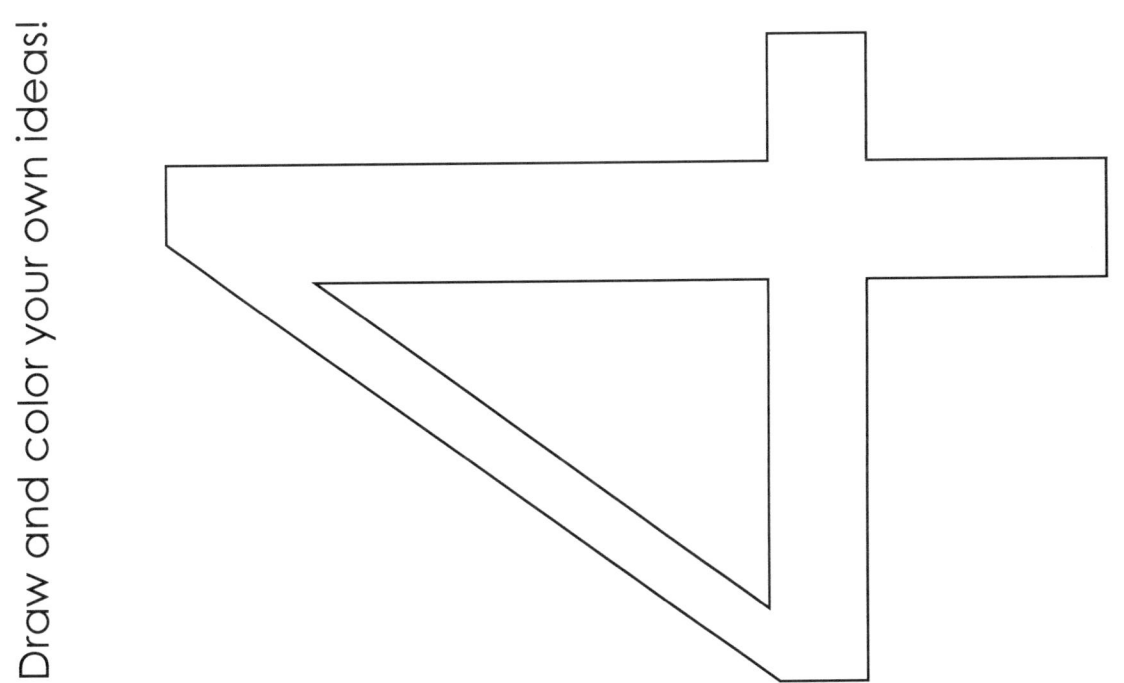

Then God said, "Let the water teem with... living creatures, and... let birds fly beneath the dome of the sky."
God saw how good it was, and God blessed them, saying, "Be fertile and multiply."
Evening came, and morning followed-
The fifth day.

5

Draw and color your own ideas!

Then God said, "Let the earth bring forth all kinds of living creatures: cattle, creeping things, and wild animals of all kinds."
    And so it happened.
    God saw how good it was.
    Then God said, "Let us make man in our image... Let them have dominion over the fish of the sea, the birds of the air, and the cattle, and over all the wild animals, and all the creatures that crawl on the ground."
    God created man in the divine image; male and female God created them.
    God blessed them saying, "Be fertile and multiply. Fill and subdue the earth."
    And so it happened.
    The Creator looked at everything that God had made and found it very good.
    Evening came, and morning followed-
        The sixth day.

22

Draw and color your own ideas!

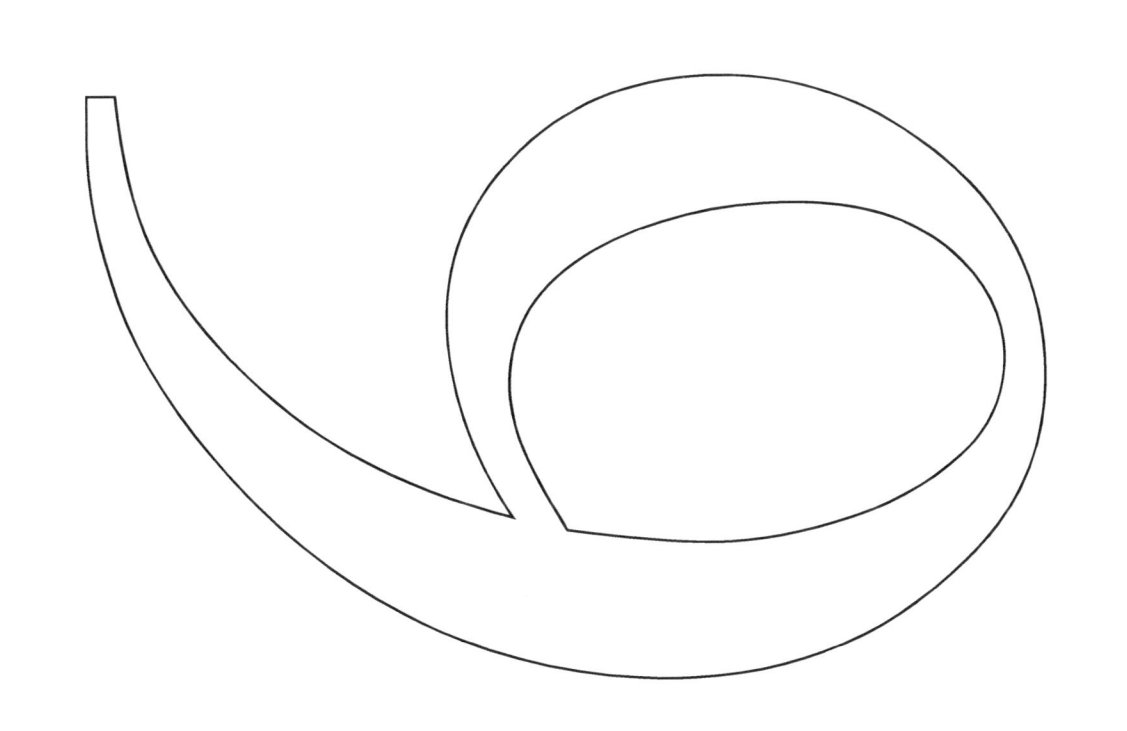

The Higher Power was finished with the work that God had been doing. God rested on the seventh day from all the work that God had undertaken.

So God blessed the seventh day and made it holy because on it God rested from all the work that was done in

CREATION.

"Such is the story of the heavens and the earth at their creation."

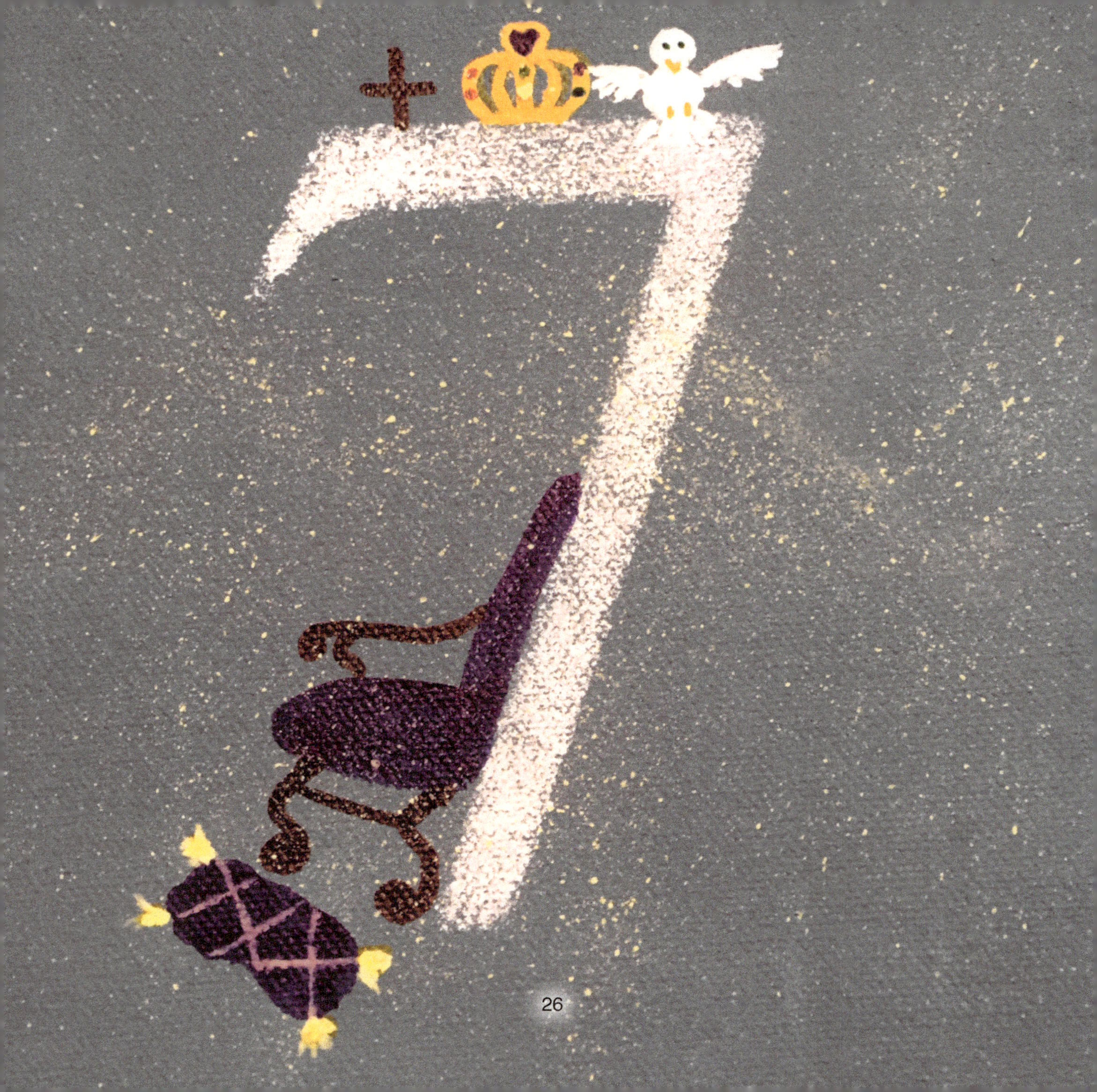

Draw and color your own ideas!

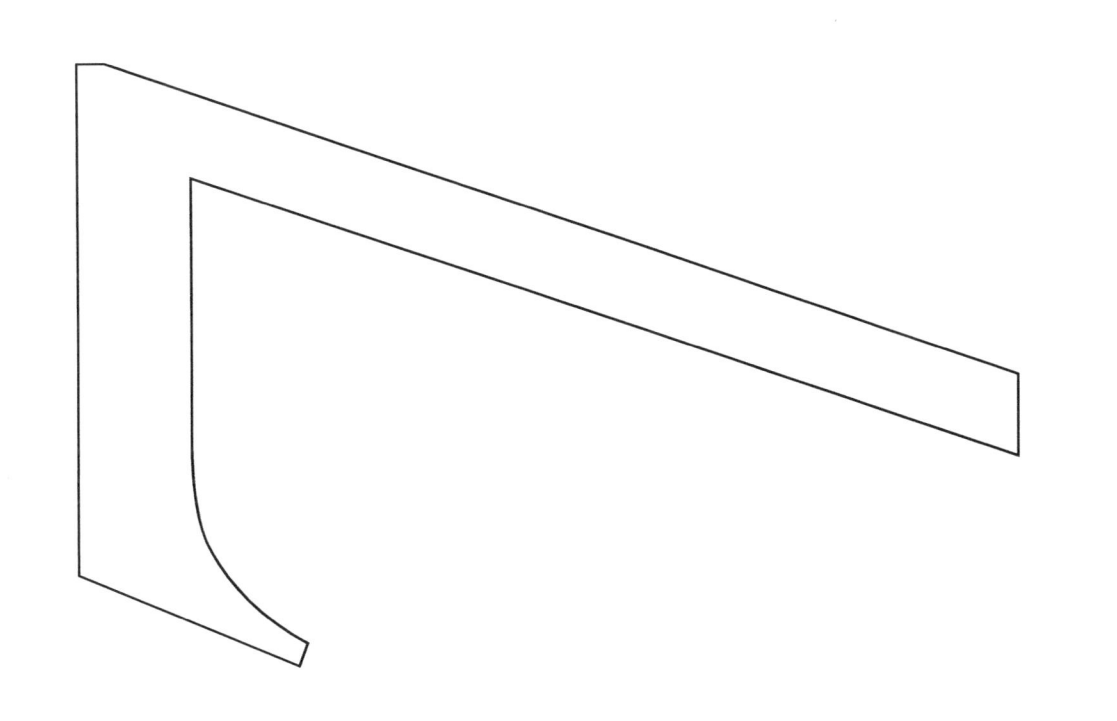

ABOUT THE AUTHOR

Joanne Semancik Krenicky Yarsevich grew up in Bethlehem, Pennsylvania, in her grandparents' house with her parents Jozie and Anna, sisters Jeanne and Rita, and brother Joseph. She attended Sts. Cyril and Methodius School and St. Francis Academy. From Cedar Crest College, Allentown, Pennsylvania, she received a BA degree in elementary education. Joanne then married Jim Yarsevich, who completed his education at UNLV. After accepting a teaching position in Clark County school district, Joanne also dabbled in drawing, sketching, and painting. Jim, taking a position with GE, took her to Kentucky,

Massachusetts, Illinois, Arizona, North Carolina, New York. She currently spends time in Clifton Park, New York, and Marana, Arizona. Their oldest son Jared married Amie Laurel Esslinger and have Freyja in Atlanta. Christopher married Rachael and have Anna and Gavin in Greenfield Center, New York. Amy lives in Troy, New York, with grand-dog Waylon. Having been an elementary school teacher and faith-formation teacher in various Catholic churches and taking classes in the Albany diocese and spiritual direction in Picture Rocks, Arizona, she always wanted to write a book. She says, "I have prepared CREATION for my grandchildren."

CPSIA information can be obtained
at www.ICGtesting.com
Printed in the USA
BVHW02e232806o618

518454BV00005B/6/P

9 781641 146807